Basic Handbook of
SmartPLS Path Modeling

Get on board easily

Dr. Saeed Behjati

Associate Prof. Dr. Siti Norezam

Published by Eastland's Science Ambassador
info@eastland-academy.com

Copyright © 2014 by saeed behjati

All right reserved: No part of this book may be reproduced or used in any form or by any means without prior written permission from the publisher.

Limit of liability/Disclaimer of Warranty: while the publisher and author have used their best efforts in preparing this book, they make no representation or warranties with respect to the accuracy, adequacy, reliability, suitability, applicability or completeness of the information contained in this book and specifically disclaim any implied warranties of merchantability or fitness for a particular purpose. No warranty may be created or extended by sales representatives or written sales materials. The statistical techniques and strategies outlined herein may not be suitable for your analysis and are not guaranteed, whether express or implied, to produce any particular result. Neither the publisher nor the author shall be liable for any damages whatsoever arising hearfrom. The techniques and ideas and suggestions are written as a general guide and that specific professional advice may be necessary.

Cover image/Design: © Saeedeh Fattahi

First edition 2014
Published by: Eastland's Science Ambassador

Preface

This book is a reader-friendly and very easy to follow for those who intend to familiarize themselves with data analysis methods. For research students, this book will provide guidelines on how easy and systematic use of statistical program of SmartPLS. Statistical technique used in the form of SmartPLS program professionally designed to estimate the variance-based structural equation.

Though the latest version of SmartPLS 3.0 is available for research fellows, and it is very much recommended by authors to advantage the latest version of this program, nevertheless, this book is written based on the previous version of SmartPLS 2.0 which can be obtained free of charge at www.smartpls.de.

The structure of this book is designed systematically begins with an a quick tour of screen , modelling and assigning data , executing (running) the analysis , factor analysis , moderation analysis , mediation and sobel test , 2nd order formative constructs , multi-group moderation and moderated mediation and how to make the reporting of the study.

This layout is easy to follow by those involved newly with the analysing research. In addition, narrative and simple language uses in this book, along with in-depth explanation of the concept using different example and set of data, helps readers within different levels of proficiency to understand the techniques and execute in their own research with confidence. Therefore, one can say, this is a real handy guide edition of statistical analysis using SmartPLS.

Acknowledgement and Dedication

The completion of this undertaking could not have been possible without assistance of many people. We are not able to list all the contributors but we value the significance of each and every contribution.

We humbly dedicate this book to our families whose untiring support and assistance have made possible the fruition of our efforts.

Saeed Behjati

Siti Norezam Othman

Authors

Dr. Saeed Behjati is a postdoctoral research scholar at the Universiti Utara Malaysia (UUM), and managing director of institute of Eastland's Science Ambassador. He is an analytic oriented academician, combining a professional sustainability portfolio in business management. He is also a technical business consultant with a precise orientation on social responsibility and ecologically sustainable development.

Dr. Siti Norezam Othman is an associate professor and senior lecturer at School of Technology Management and Logistics in Universiti Utara Malaysia. She has been lecturing subjects related to Operations Management such as Management Science, System of Design, Procurement and Supply Chain for undergraduate and Operations Technology Management for postgraduate students. Her research interests include Sustainable Operations Management, Technology Sustainability, Halal and sustainability and other sustainability related subjects.

Content

	Preface	iii
	Acknowledgement and Dedication	iv
	Authors	v
	Introduction	1
Chapter 1	A Quick Tour of Screen	5
Chapter 2	Modelling and Assigning Data	13
Chapter 3	Executing (Running) the Analysis	17
Chapter 4	Factor Analysis	25
Chapter 5	Moderation Analysis	34
Chapter 6	Mediation and Sobel Test	39
Chapter 7	2nd Order Formative Constructs	45
Chapter 8	Multigroup Moderation and Moderated Mediation	51
	Reference	62
	Index	63

Introduction

SmartPLS is one of the leading statistical software applications uses to estimate more complex models with a smaller amount of data, because it is not working based on covariance matrix. Particularly, the PLS-SEM is more preferred when the data are not normally distributed, or the model is complex and basically constructed to estimate variety of indicators and relationships. Despite of these attribute, let's begins with this explanation that smart-PLS is not uses only because it has the power of analysing and accept the small sample size; or because the distributed data is not normal; or because the research model is conceptually complex. It might be only one good reason for justification of using PLS which is the factors relationship in constructed research model.

Mostly among early researcher, a lot of time allocating to develop the research model (framework) and then spend even more time on constructs and the relationship between constructs, while in between they ignore sometime the importance of the measurement of these constructs. Particularly, in structural equation modelling, the constructs create the structural model and the measures make the measurement model, hence if there is any problem with the measurement, consequently the issue will lead to structural model and the research fails.

It is reminding that, measurement model shows the relationship between a latent variable and its measured items (variables); and structural Models specify models in SEM in which, the straight arrows represent direct effects; curved arrows represent bidirectional "correlational" relationships; ellipses represent latent variables and also boxes/rectangles represent observed variables.

Basically, there are two different model of relationship between construct and measure of 'Formative' and 'Reflective' measurement model.

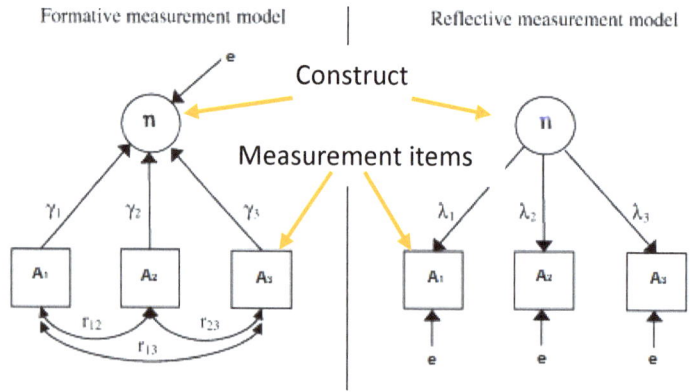

In 'reflective model' it is the construct that caused the changes in measurement items (which sometimes also called indicators or items) while in case of 'formative model' it is the role of measurement item that caused the change in construct. The arrows in each form also indicates the changes coming from/to measurement items and construct.

Noted that, in case of 'reflective measurement model', the correlation between the indicators should be high, while in case of 'formative measurement model' the construct validity has more priority. In fact, some researchers says that these measurement indicators (items) in 'formative model' should have as low correlation as possible. In other word, while reflective indicators are essentially interchangeable means that they are highly correlated (and therefore, the removal of an item does not change the essential nature of the underlying construct), in contrary in 'formative indicators' omitting an indicator is omitting a part of the construct meaning that these indicators are very distinct from each other.

We can also see that measure conflict between these two perspectives, in rule of theory approach. In reflective model, we should develop theory of the relationship between constructs and use those theories to shape how data will be collected, whereas in case of formative model, we should look at patterns in data and let the data provide the basis of the theories.

Some sort of questions can help to distinguish these two different perspective.

Scale Type	Reflective	Formative
Are the indicators defining characteristics of the construct?	No (representative sample)	Yes (complete inventory)
Do changes in the indicators cause changes in the construct?	No	Yes
Do changes in the constructs cause changes in the indicators?	Yes	No
Do the indicators necessarily share a common theme? (internal consistency)	Yes	No
Does eliminating one indicator alter the conceptual domain of the construct?	No	Yes
Is a change in one indicator necessarily associated with a change in all other indicators?	Yes	No
Do the indicators have the same antecedents and consequences?	Yes	No

In conclude it is note that, among variety of statistical practises, SEM-PLS is powerful statistical techniques for 'Formative Constructs'. With this introduction, in next we begins explaining the SmartPLS in details which is break into 8 chapters.

Chapter 1

A Quick Tour of Screen

Learning Objectives:

This chapter offers understanding about:

- Basic feature of software package
- Start a new project, and load data
- Troubleshooting data entry

This is an introduction chapter which is discuss about the basic feature of PLS, how to start a new project, and load and troubleshooting data entry.

The first step is of course, start and open the Smart-PLS software from your computer. The following screenshot demonstrates the blanked windows of the ver2.0 of this program.

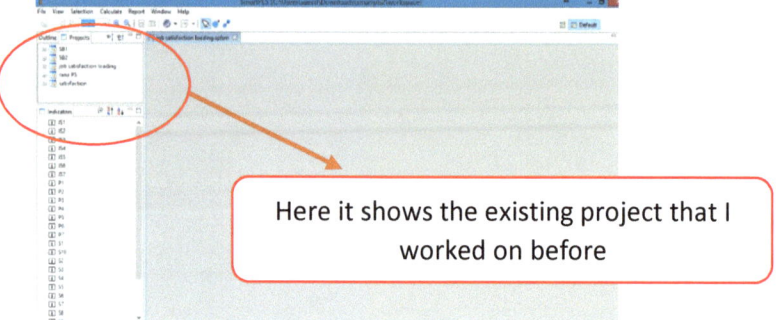

Here it shows the existing project that I worked on before

To start a **New Project**, go to menu bar and from the tab of 'File' select the option of "New" and then 'Create New Project".

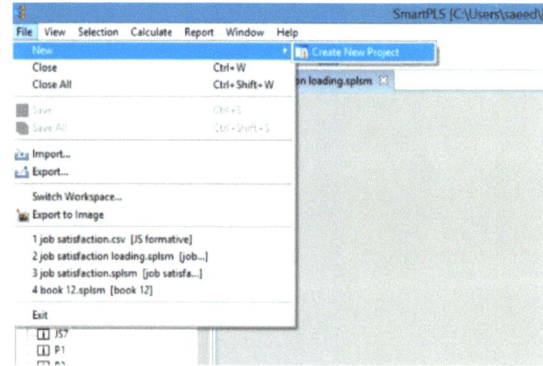

And from the open up windows "Create a Project" type your project name and then "Next".

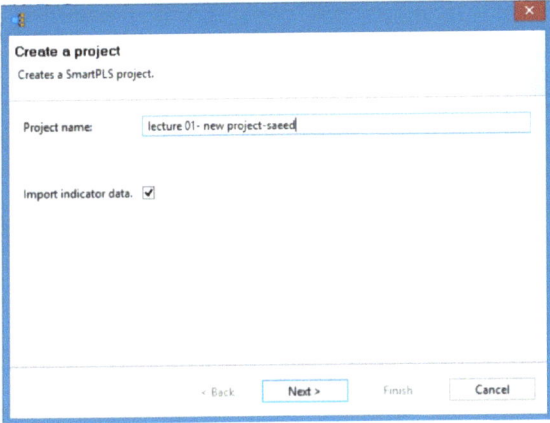

In new pop-up windows, you need to indicate the path to a file which contains your research indicator data. The new project is now added in our working project.

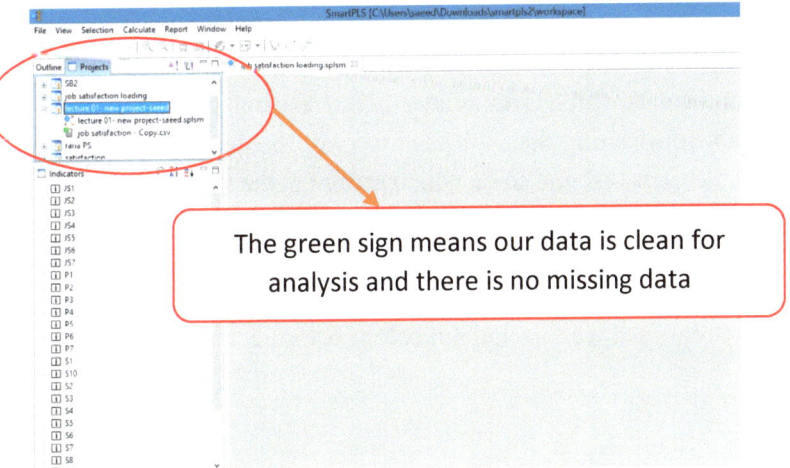

The green sign means our data is clean for analysis and there is no missing data

Reminder:

PLS is only accept certain format of data. It should be either with CSV or TXT format to be able to read by PLS.

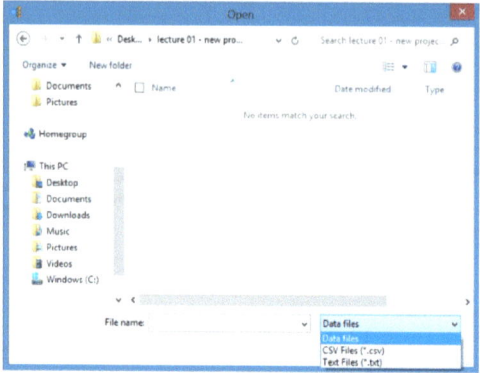

What we need to do, is convert our excel file sheet to the CSV format.

Perhaps, it is also important to note, PLS is very sensitive about the data which is not related to the research model and variables. Meaning that, we need to omit the demographic variables, case ID and so on which are not in the framework.

Lastly, PLS does not handle blanked cells and missing data. In other word, if our data is not clean, instead of green sign on our data set, we face the red colour warning.

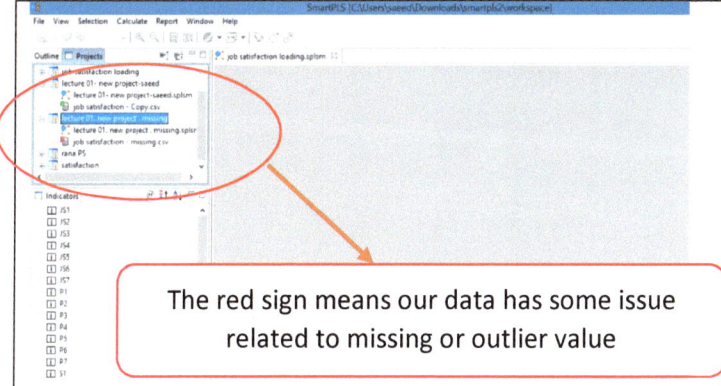

The red sign means our data has some issue related to missing or outlier value

The easy way is let the PLS to solve this issue.
1. Double click on data set
2. Choose the option of "comma" and then
3. Validate the data set

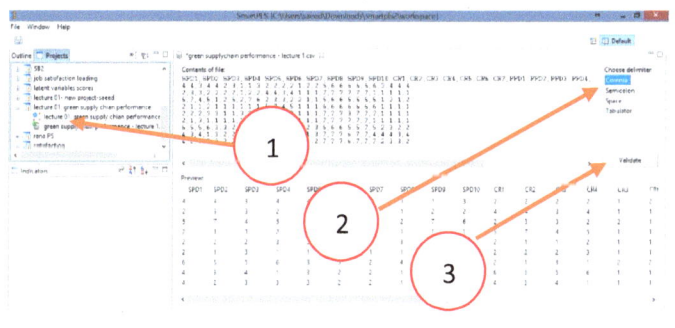

Alternative slouation is to find the problem in our data and solve it. To do that we use the SPSS, and proceed the Analysis → Descriptive Statistics → Frequencies …

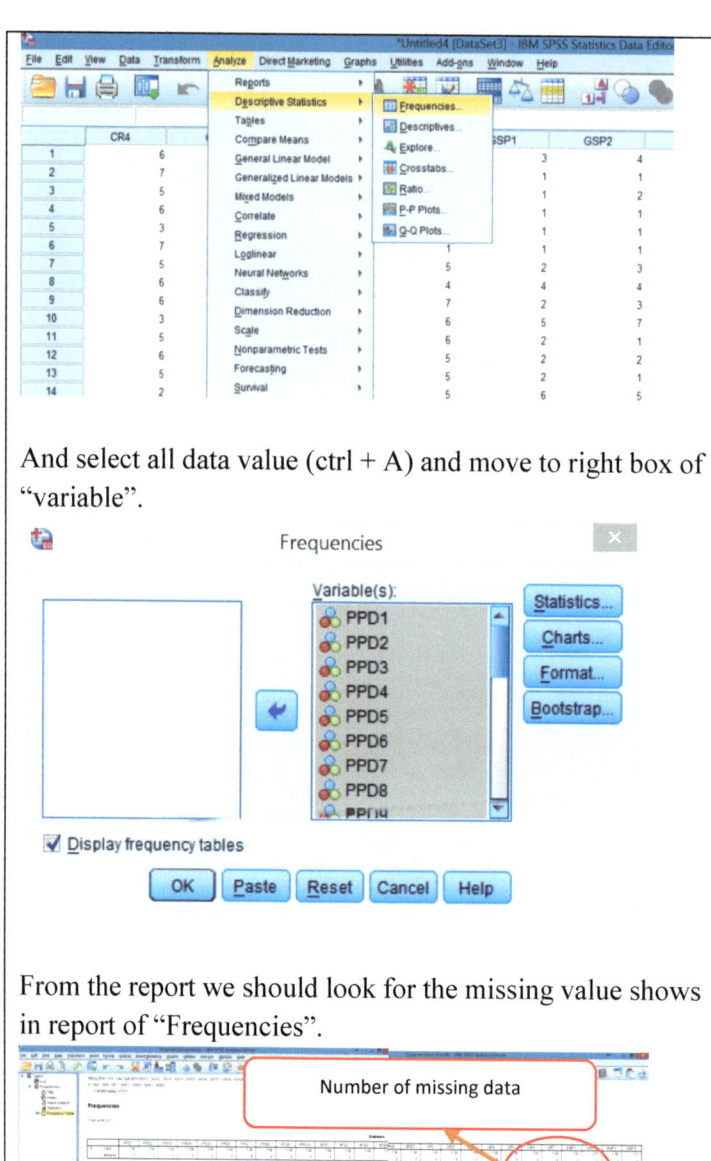

And select all data value (ctrl + A) and move to right box of "variable".

From the report we should look for the missing value shows in report of "Frequencies".

Number of missing data

To transform the missing values, we proceeds the:
Transorm ➔ Replacing Missing Values..

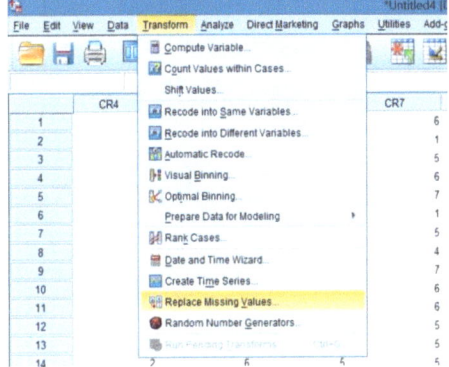

From the pop-up windows, we select the items which we discover they have missing value. We need to select these items once per time.

As it shows in following screenshot,
    1. Change the name of this item (we change it to GSP2_corrected).
    2. The method of transformation is defined as "median of nearby point" because the data is in interval scale of 7 point Likert.
    3. Select the " All" missing value to be span of nearby points
    4. Click on " Change"
    5. Ok

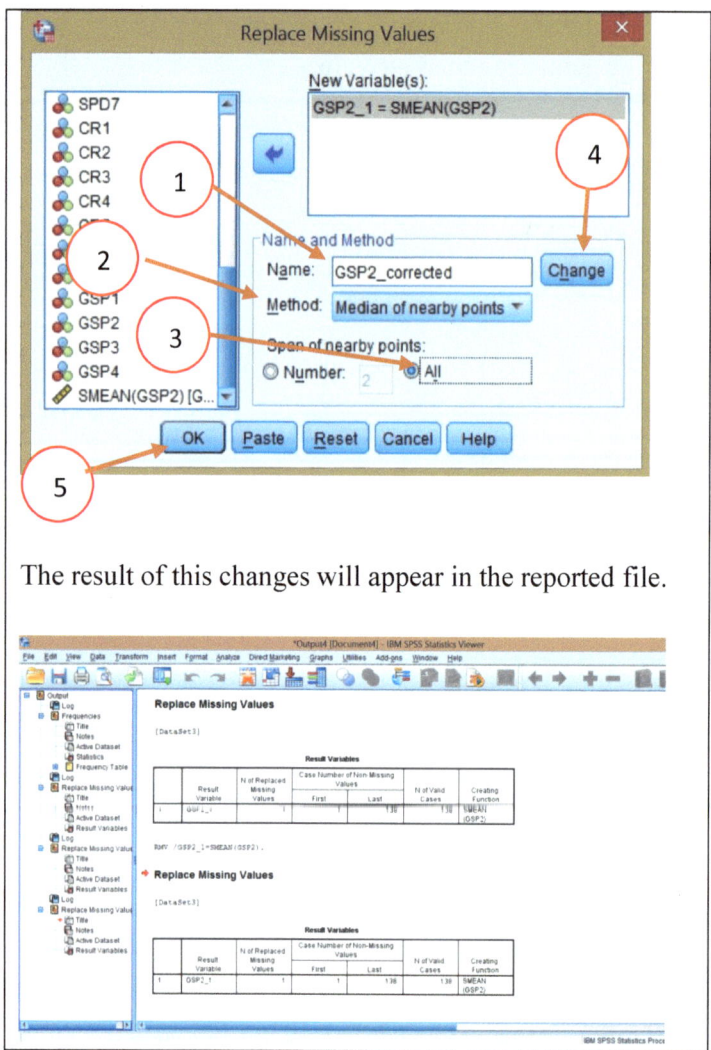

The result of this changes will appear in the reported file.

Now it is time to modelling our data, which will be detail in next part.

Chapter 2

Modelling and Assigning Data

Learning Objectives:

This chapter offers understanding about:

- Step-wise modelling
- Initiate the path analysis

To do modelling, let us consider an example related to research about "Green Supply Chain Performance". The conceptual framework of this research is drafted bellow.

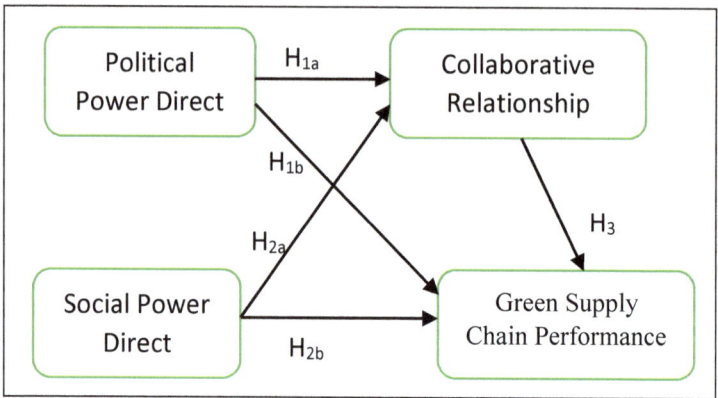

The first step is to draft the variables and their connection. Three drawing tool are given for this purpose. And as it demonstrated through the following screenshot:

    1. The arrows to move around the tools, select and deselection of icons.

    2. Construct maker. This is an insertion mode and uses for assigning the factors (variables)

    3. This tools is uses to stablish the connection between factors (variables)

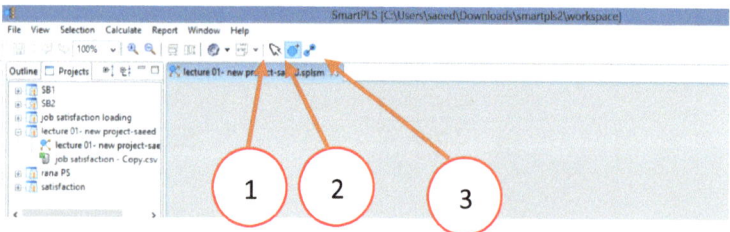

By using these tools, we sketched the model. And by easy way of drag and drop, we select the dimensions and assign them to each factors.

Reminder:

By right click on assigned factors (variable), some other options are provided, such as rename or deleting the variables and also aligning the items in rotate them to fit into our page.

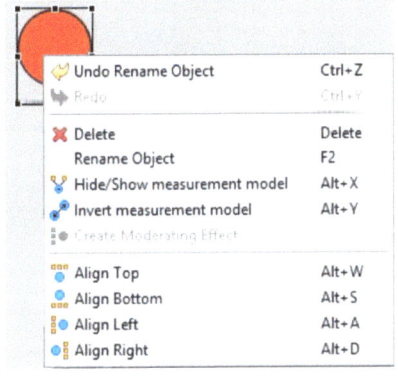

Noted that, the red colour of our factor is because still we didn't assign the relationship between the factors. And though the model in this stage can be uses for factor analysis, but it is unable to execute the path analysis.

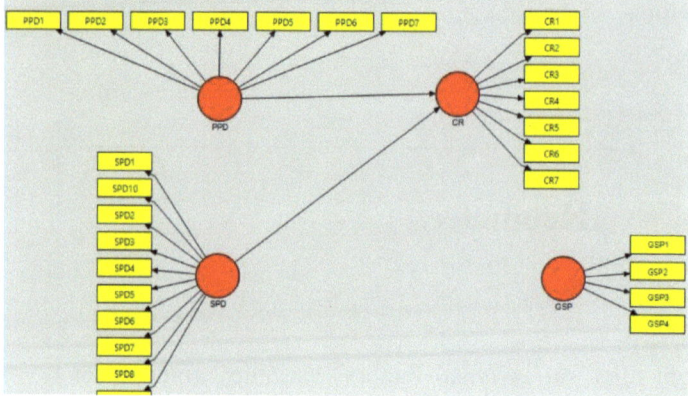

As we mentioned, after drawing the model and establish the relationship between the factors, the colour of factors from red will turn to blue which it means the model is ready for analysis.

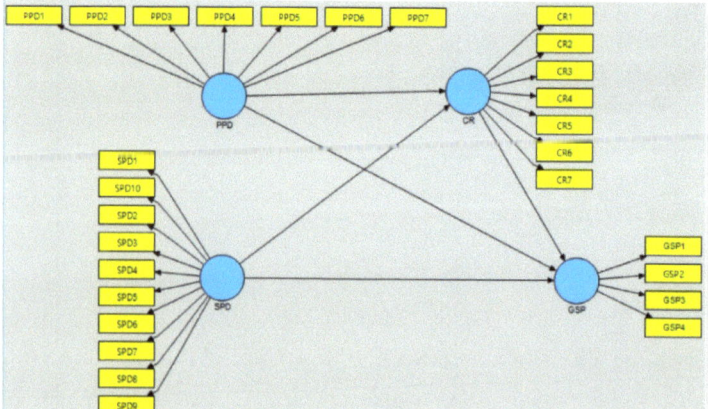

Chapter 3

Executing (Running) the Analysis

Learning Objectives:

This chapter offers understanding about:

- Step-wise process of executing PLS path analysis
- The analysis of PLS algorithm and bootstrapping

3.1. Path Analysis:

For proceed the *PLS Path Analysis*, we can either choose the easy icon of "PLS Algorithm" available on screen or through menu bar:

Calculate ➔ PLS Algorithm

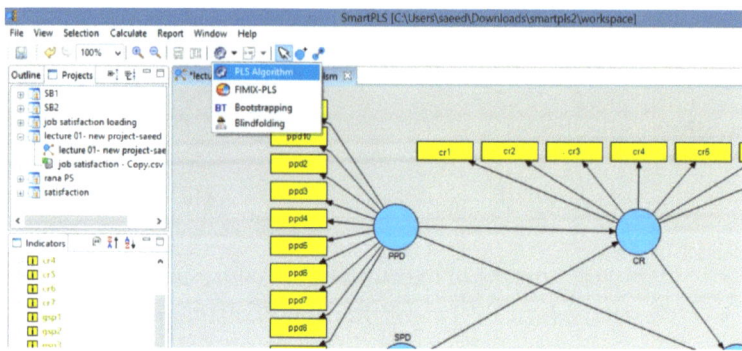

After PLS calculation, the results will present in term of values shown on each construct relation. In which:
1. Standardized Regression Weights
2. Factor Loading
3. R-squared*

* R-Square - This is the proportion of variance explained by the explanatory variables

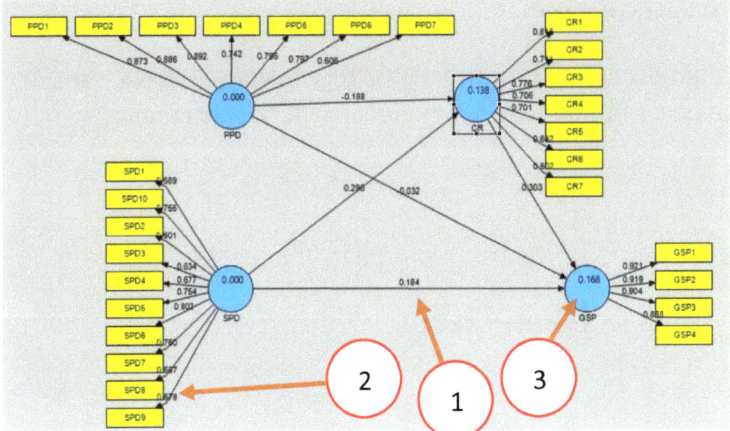

Noted that, the factor loading which are the extended correlation are expected to be greater than 0.7 on average.

In order to find whether, these loading are significant, we need to execute the "Bootstrapping".

3.2. Bootstrapping:

To find the answer of whether "Regression Weights" are significance or not, we need to proceed the "bootstrapping".

Reminder:

The basic idea of bootstrapping is resampling which is allows estimation of the sampling distribution, using random sampling methods.

One goal of this techniques is to determine the value of a parameter of a population, which is typically too expensive or even impossible to measure. Therefore, We sample a population, measure a statistic of this sample, and then use this statistic to say something about the corresponding parameter of the population.

Let us consider this explanation through a manufacturing example. Supposed to we measure the mean weight of our produced chocolate. We use sampling techniques and randomly choose 100 chocolate and calculate the mean of these sample and generalize the mean of our sample to the entire population within a margin of error our sample. The question is what if after couple of months later we were in need to know with greater accuracy - or less of a margin of error - what the mean of our chocolate weight was on the day that we sampled the production line. Of course we cannot use today's sample as too many variables have entered the picture and also we don't have a time machine back to that day and resample again.

Fortunately we can use the technique of bootstrapping, using a computer, and randomly sample with replacement from the 100 known weights and form a new sample (called a 'resample' or bootstrap sample) This process is repeated a large number of times (typically, 500, 1,000 or 10,000 times), and for each of these bootstrap samples we compute its mean (each of these are called bootstrap estimates). We now have a histogram of bootstrap means, which is provides an estimate of the shape of the distribution of the mean from which we can answer questions about how much the mean varies. (The method here, described for the mean, can be applied to almost any other statistic or estimator.)

Adèr et al. recommend the bootstrap procedure for the following situations:

- When the theoretical distribution of a statistic of interest is complicated or unknown. Since the bootstrapping procedure is distribution-independent it provides an indirect method to assess the properties of the distribution underlying the sample and the parameters of interest that are derived from this distribution.
- When the sample size is insufficient for straightforward statistical inference. If the underlying distribution is well-known, bootstrapping provides a way to account for the

> distortions caused by the specific sample that may not be fully representative of the population.
> - When power calculations have to be performed, and a small pilot sample is available. Most power and sample size calculations are heavily dependent on the standard deviation of the statistic of interest. If the estimate used is incorrect, the required sample size will also be wrong. One method to get an impression of the variation of the statistic is to use a small pilot sample and perform bootstrapping on it to get impression of the variance.

To do bootstrapping in PLS we can either choose the "Bootstrapping: from the easy access of screen icons or through the PLS menu bar:

Calculate ➔ Bootstrapping

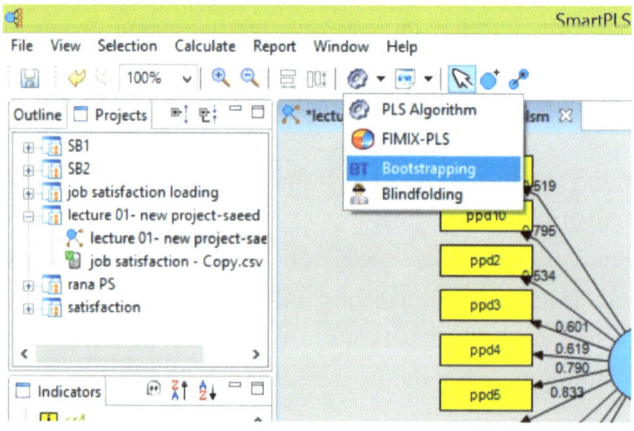

From the pup-window, we should indicate the number of our cases in research. And then, we will allow the PLS to run the model with 500 samples, or even more sample size.

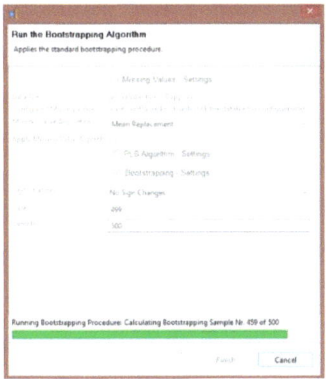

As it shows in screenshot of Bootstrap, instead of "Regression Weights" now we have the value of "t-statistics", which uses as indication of significance. As such, any value greater than 1.96 is significant at the point 0.5 level or %95 of confidence level.

✋ Noted that, when the sample size is small, because typically we don't have enough power to achieve significance, therefore we can increase the Bootstrap number, which is by increasing the reliable estimate, subsequently, the t-statistics will increase and, the error and the p-value will decrease.

As it shows in our example model, hypothesis H_{1b} (the relation between "political power drivers" and "green supply chain performance") looks is rejected while the strongest relation exposed between "social power drivers" and the "collaborative relationship".

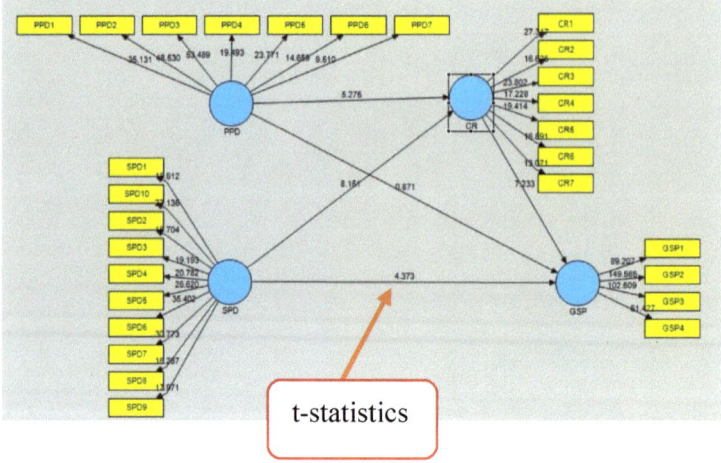

t-statistics

Chapter 2

Factor Analysis

Learning Objectives:

This chapter offers understanding about:

- Step-wise process of factor analysis

To explain the process of factor analysis, let's have an example of basic model for job satisfaction. As it shows in research framework the study is about the different factors associated with job satisfaction which are eventually leading to turnover.

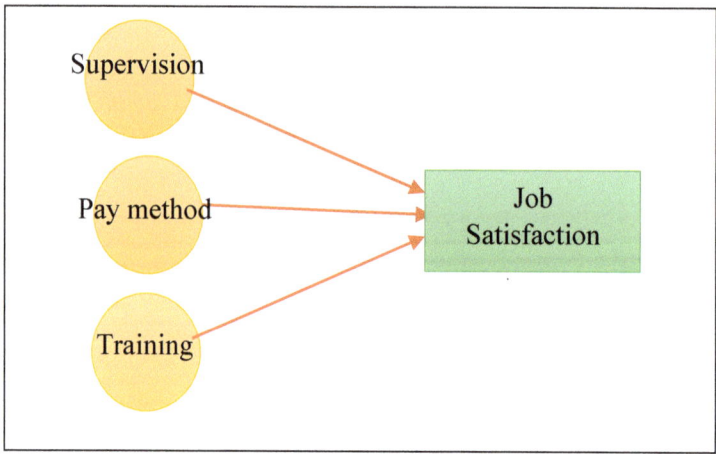

The basic model sketched in PLS presented in following figure.

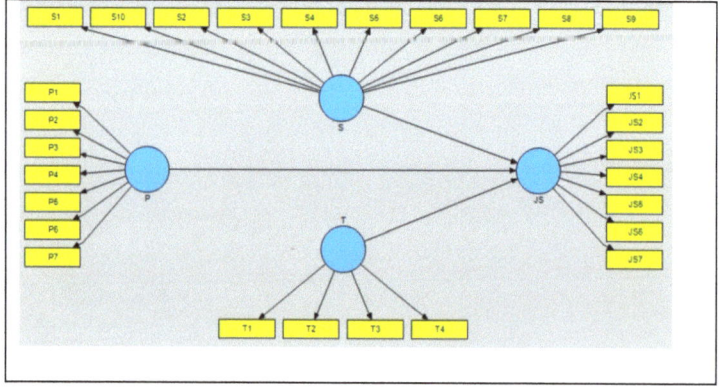

As it seen in model, we have 4 factors and each with several indicators. To run the model we proceeds:

Calculate ➔ PLS algorithm

And from pop-up window, we keep the default options and just press "Finish". PLS calculate the model and presented the following loading model.

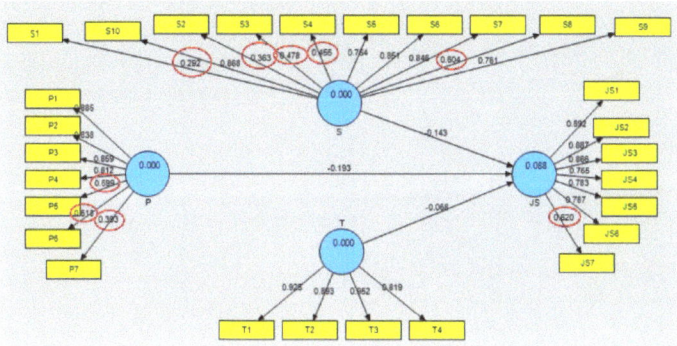

✋ Noted that all relations in this model are reflective constructs. Thus the values shows are 'loading' values. While if our variables have formative constructs, then the given values will be 'weighs' rather than loading.

The aim of loading is to average out about 0.7 and more for every factors. And as we see in our example 8 item of P6, P7, P5, S1, S2, S3, S4 and S8 have some issues and not reaching to our accepted range.

One way we could do to solve this issue is simply remove these items one at the time. Because for this factor there are all reflective items which means they are interchangeable, basically explaining the same issue, thus replacing or removing one should not effects on our entire model.

So in our example, we delete one item "the lowest one" and we run the model once again. And we continue deleting the items until the results shows all loading are above 0.7 and we obtain an accepted measurement model.

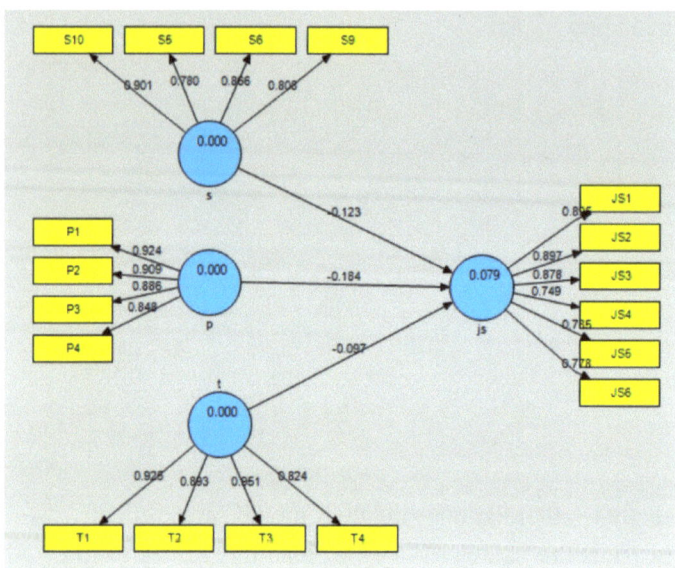

Next step is to check the report of PLS. The procedure is:

Report ➔ Html (print) report

From the report, to initiates lets the reports of "Outer Loading" been present.

PLS ➔ Calculation Results ➔ Outer Loading

Table of contents (complete)

- Model
    - Specification
        - Measurement Model Specification
        - Manifest Variable Scores (Original)
        - Structural Model Specification
- PLS
    - Quality Criteria
        - Overview
        - Redundancy
        - Cronbachs Alpha
        - Latent Variable Correlations
        - R Square
        - Cross Loadings
        - AVE
        - Communality
        - Total Effects
        - Composite Reliability
    - Calculation Results
        - Stop Criterion Changes
        - **← Outer Loadings**
        - Outer Model (Weights or Loadings)
        - Path Coefficients
        - Latent Variable Scores
        - Manifest Variable Scores (Used)
        - Outer Weights
- Data Preprocessing
    - Results (chronologically)
        - Step 0 (Original Matrix)
- Index Values
    - Results
        - Measurement Model (restandardised)
        - Path Coefficients
        - Measurement Model
        - Latent Variable Scores (unstandardised)
        - Index Values for Latent Variables

Outer loading

	js	p	s	t
JS1	0.895366			
JS2	0.89703			
JS3	0.8781			
JS4	0.748734			
JS5	0.78505			
JS6	0.777551			
P1		0.923745		
P2		0.909273		
P3		0.885897		
P4		0.848118		
S10			0.901408	
S5			0.779857	
S6			0.865663	
S9			0.807859	
T1				0.924829
T2				0.892581
T3				0.951271
T4				0.823574

As we see in this report we have accepted factor loading. Perhaps the next step is to check the "Cross Loading" for discriminant validity purpose. Thus, from the report:

PLS ➔ Quality Criteria ➔ Cross Loading

To present the result it is commonly preferred to sort the result in Excel through conditional formatting for value greater than 0.5.

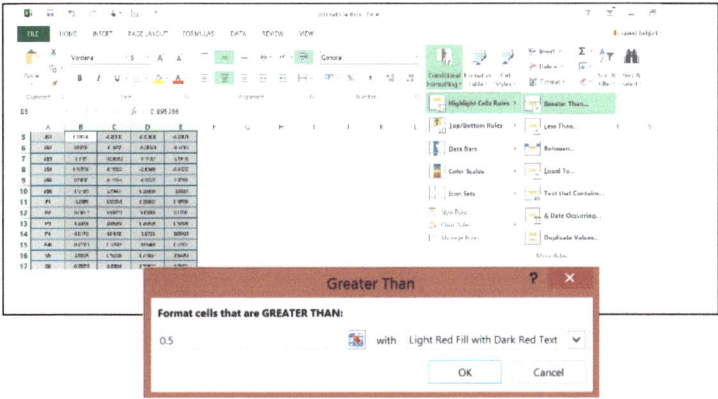

Cross Loadings

	js	p	s	t
JS1	0.895366	-0.209183	-0.230838	-0.122674
JS2	0.89703	-0.19257	-0.215639	-0.114564
JS3	0.8781	-0.268652	-0.117031	-0.194733
JS4	0.748734	-0.119026	-0.189419	-0.146263
JS5	0.78505	-0.121344	-0.00527	-0.072881

JS6	0.777551	-0.134477	0.005684	-0.03053
P1	-0.20155	0.923745	0.206863	0.185788
P2	-0.236412	0.909273	0.159706	0.117093
P3	-0.20699	0.885897	0.256505	0.159976
P4	-0.134713	0.848118	0.12728	0.099425
S10	-0.177075	0.143567	0.901408	0.145852
S5	-0.119375	0.150338	0.779857	0.354853
S6	-0.175575	0.191804	0.865663	0.180831
S9	-0.135293	0.244388	0.807859	0.128128
T1	-0.111504	0.164383	0.207191	0.924829
T2	-0.090387	0.106243	0.245455	0.892581
T3	-0.203232	0.140681	0.187115	0.951271
T4	-0.050209	0.205798	0.242226	0.823574

As we see there is no major cross loadings.

Noted that, the basic procedures of path analysis is same as well. Let's consider the model presented in following

screenshot, which is contains formative construct as well. Here we have:
1. Values of reflective measurement are 'factor loading'.
2. Values of formative measurement are 'factor Weights'.

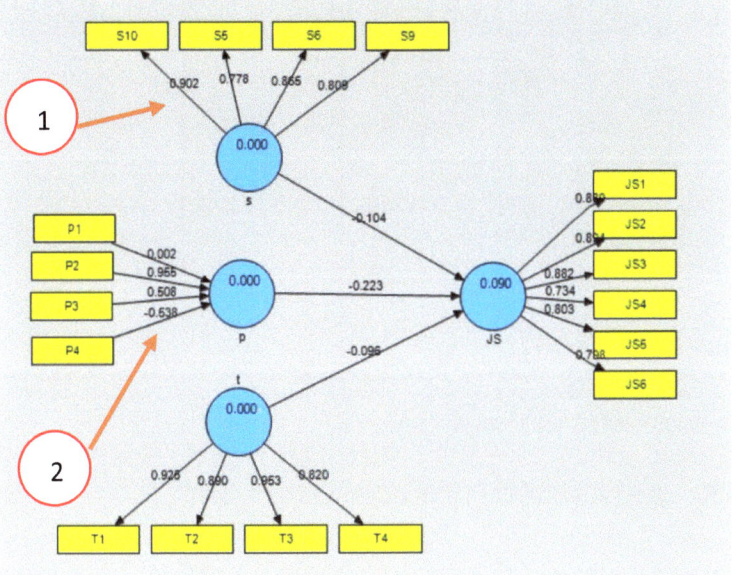

Chapter 5

Moderation Analysis

Learning Objectives:

This chapter offers understanding about:

- Step-wise process of moderation analysis

There are two different type of moderation, 'Multi-group Moderation' and 'Interaction Moderation'.

Here we explain the Interaction Moderation through the research related to "Green Supply Chain Performance". The model construct is shows in following framework. We like to test whether it is interaction between "Political Power Drivers" and "Social Power Drivers" in such a way increasing one changes the relation of other variable and dependent variable.

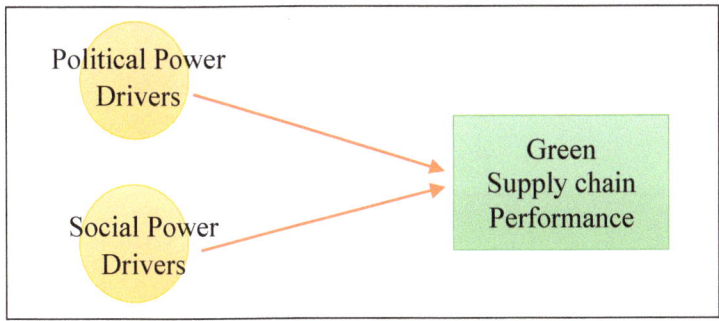

The concept of "Interaction Moderation" is to multiply all indicators of each variable together.

The procedures in PLS is to right click on DV and select the "Crate Moderating Effect" and then from the pop up form, specify the moderator and predictor variables. And also chose the mode of interaction effect.

As it exposed through following screenshot, we were interested to find interaction moderation effect of "Political Power Drivers" on "Social Power Drivers".

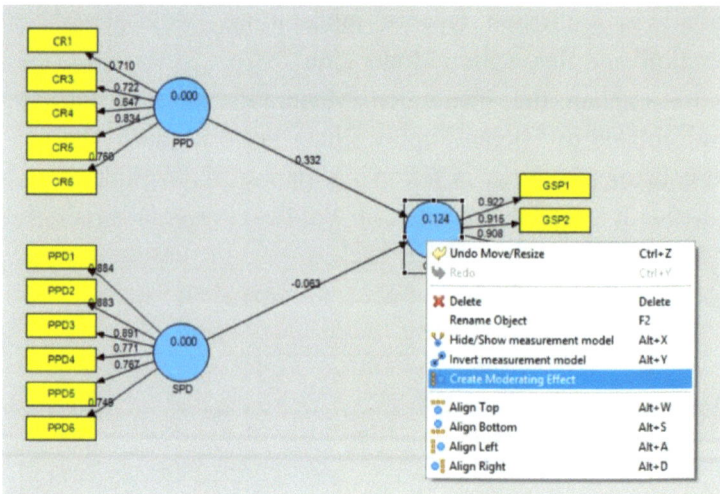

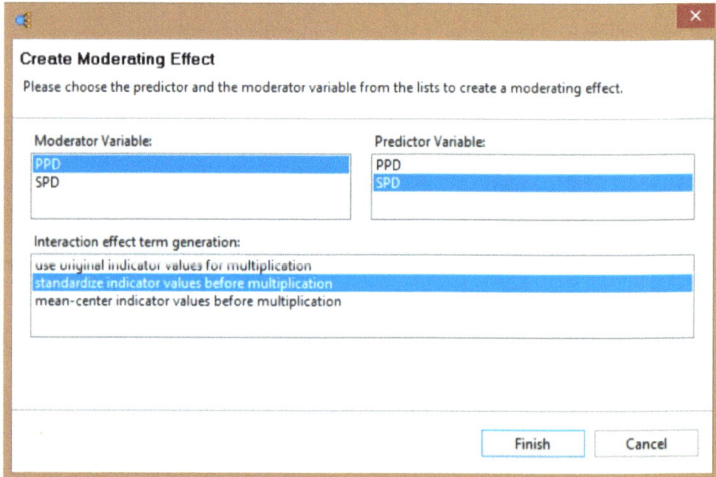

The next screenshot, shows the added interaction moderation by PLS.

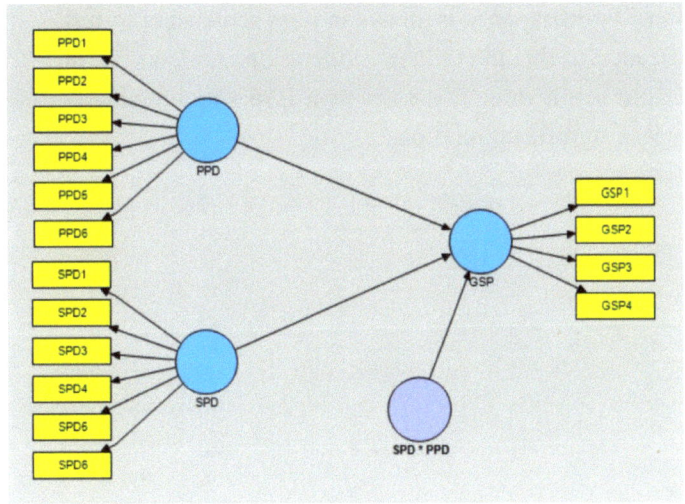

The next step is to run the analysis.
Calculate ➔ PLS algorithm

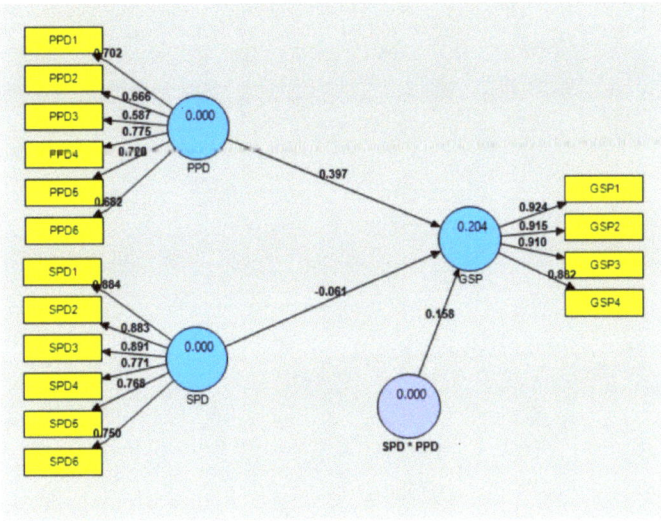

The result of bootstrapping is shows in next screenshot to test the significance of this interaction moderation. As it shows in number 1, our result value is greater than 1.96 which indicates definitely it is significant relations.

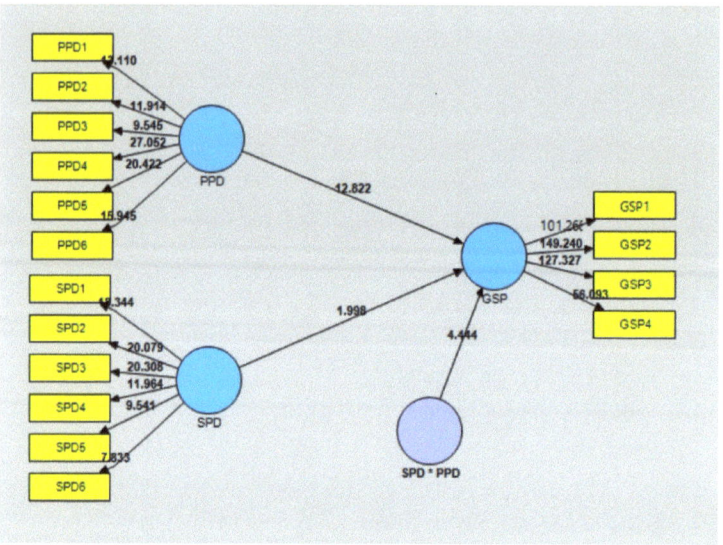

Chapter 6

Mediation and Sobel test

Learning Objectives:

This chapter offers understanding about:

- Step-wise process of mediation analysis

Let's consider a basic mediation example of "Green Supply Chain Performance" where the "collaborative relationship' is mediating the "social power drivers" and "green supply chain performance".

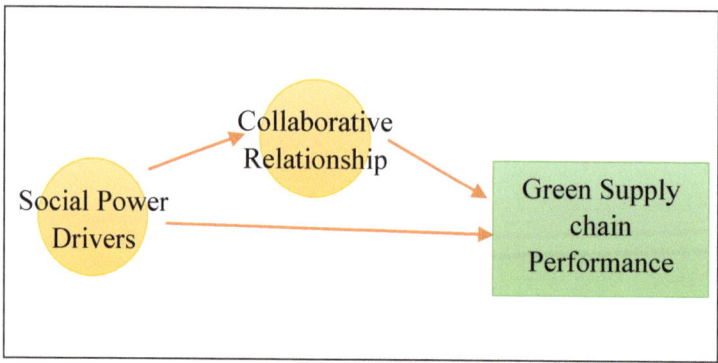

Here we need to extract some values, in order to test the "sobel Test".

Direct value with Mediator	0.363
Direct value with No Mediator	0.407
IV → Med Beta	- 0.229703
Med → DV Beta	- 0.043985
IV → Med Standard error	0.037439
Med → DV Standard error	0.034246

The required data which presented in table are extracted from running the PLS and bootstrapping analysis and presented through following screenshots.

The first screenshot is PLS algorithm, which gives us the value

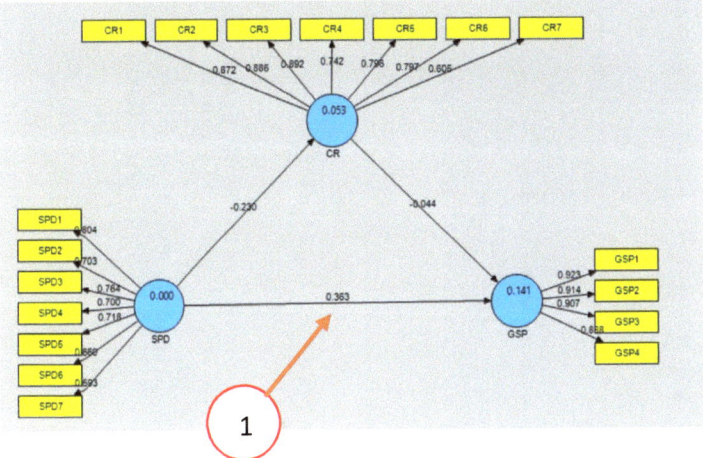

Next screenshot shows the PLS algorithm values without effect of mediator.

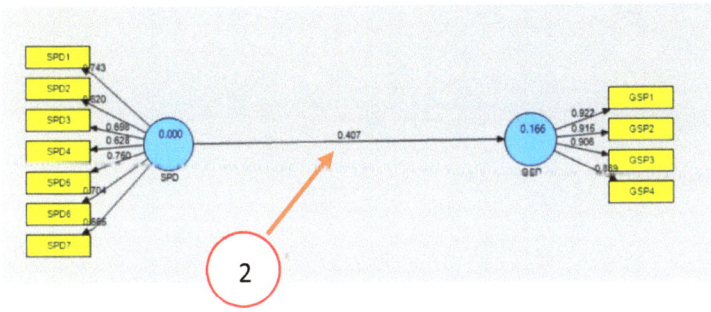

Following screenshot shows the bootstrap values.

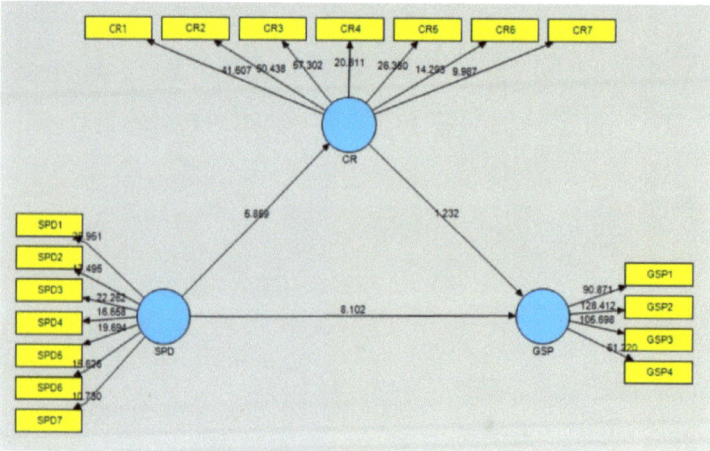

We need to extract the values from the report of

Bootstrapping ➔ Path Coefficients (Mean, STDEV, T-Values)

Table of contents (complete)

- Bootstrapping
    - Bootstrapping
        - Outer Weights
        - Inner Model T-Statistic
        - Path Coefficients
        - Total Effects (Mean, STDEV, T-Values)
        - Outer Model T-Statistic
        - Path Coefficients (Mean, STDEV, T-Values) ⇐
        - Outer Weights (Mean, STDEV, T-Values)
        - Total Effects
        - Outer Loadings
        - Outer Loadings (Mean, STDEV, T-Values)
- Model
    - Specification
        - Measurement Model Specification
        - Manifest Variable Scores (Original)
        - Structural Model Specification
- Data Preprocessing
    - Results (chronologically)
        - Step 0 (Original Matrix)

Path Coefficients (Mean, STDEV, T-Values)

	Original Sample (O)	Sample Mean (M)	Standard Deviation (STDEV)	Standard Error (STERR)
CR -> GSP	-0.043985	-0.047748	0.034246	0.034246
SPD -> CR	-0.229703	-0.236651	0.037439	0.037439
SPD -> GSP	0.363306	0.364085	0.046359	0.046359

	T Statistics (|O/STERR|)
CR -> GSP	1.284396
SPD -> CR	6.135413
SPD -> GSP	7.836879

③ ④ ⑤ ⑥

The next step is to take extracted values to online Sobel Test, derived from:
http://www.danielsoper.com/statcalc3/calc.aspx?id=31

The purpose of Sobel test is to test whether a mediator carries the influence of an IV to a DV.

The next screenshot is giving the result of "Sobel test".

Sobel test statistic:	1.23019174
One-tailed probability:	0.10931266
Two-tailed probability:	0.21862531

The "Sobel test statistic" should be with absolute value greater than 1.96 and also the value of "Two-tailed probability" should be less than 0.05 for %95 confidence.

In our example the Sobel test statistic is 1.2301 and the Two-tailed probability shows the value of 0.2186. Therefore, we can conclude that, in our example the mediator does partially mediate the effect between the IV and DV. Because, though the direct effect with no mediator (0.407) did decreased the strength of Direct value with Mediator (0.363); nevertheless the t-statistic value of 8.012 (revealed by bootstrapping) is still significant as it is greater than 1.96. Thus we have partial mediation.

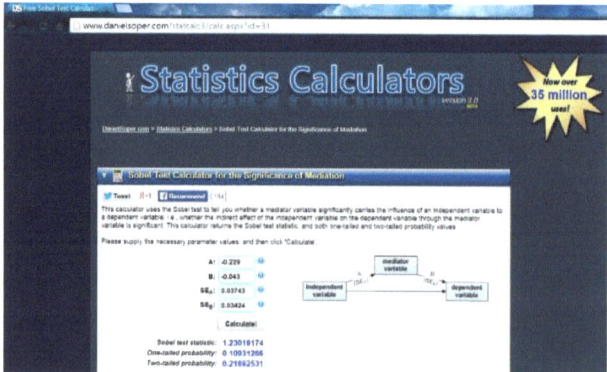

Chapter 7

2nd order Formative Constructs

Learning Objectives:

This chapter offers understanding about:

- Basic model of second order formative structure

PLS, has two phase approach for second order formative structure. Let us consider the "green supply chain performance" as an example. The following screenshot is the research conceptual framework; and as it shows in framework:
1. First Order
2. Second Order

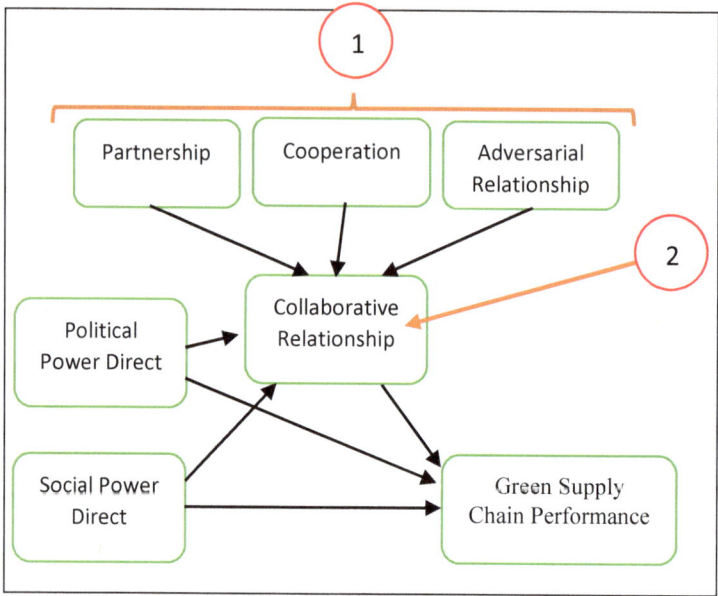

Based on our model we have 2 indicators for each first order factors; and also total 6 indicators for second order factors. These indicators were hide for presenting better the values of our model.

The first phase, we proceed the PLS algorithm as it shows through the following screenshot.

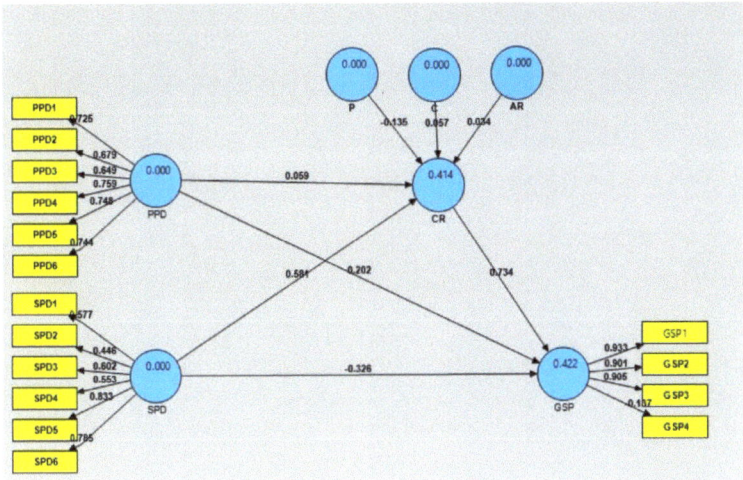

The next step is to from "Default Report" choose the "Latent Variable Scores" from the "PLS Calculation Results"

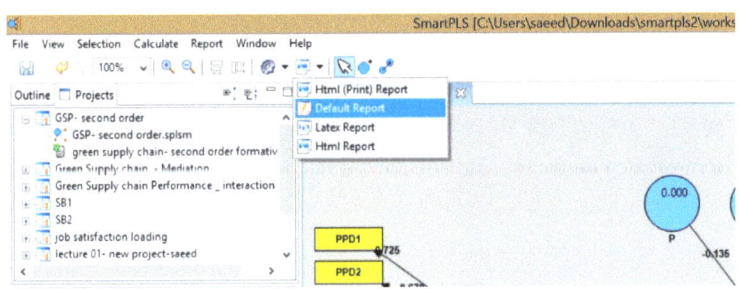

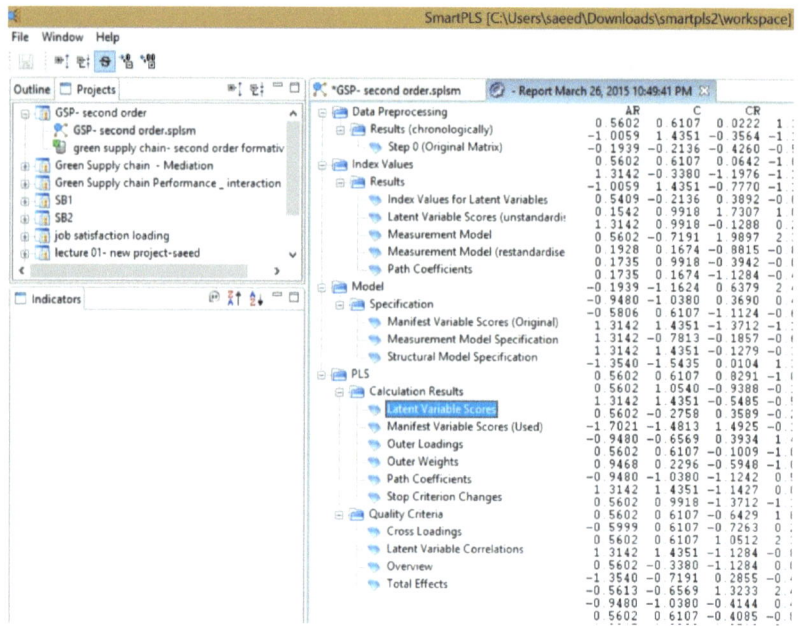

This report produced scores for all the latent variables. What we need to do is select all values and copy them to Excel, while we do need to keep only the values for second orders.

	A	B	C	D	E	F	G
1	P	AR	C	CR	GSP	PPD	SPD
2	0.2352	0.5602	0.6107	0.0222	1.3879	0.7042	-0.4244
3	1.148	-1.0059	1.4351	-0.3564	-1.1213	-0.6409	0.5489
4	0.2352	-0.1939	-0.2136	-0.426	-0.5705	0.7136	1.4612
5	0.2352	0.5602	0.6107	0.0642	-1.0941	-1.5871	1.1736
6	1.148	1.3142	-0.338	-1.1976	-1.1213	-0.6444	-0.5094
7	1.148	-1.0059	1.4351	-0.777	-1.1213	-1.4931	-1.0193
8	0.2352	0.5409	-0.2136	0.3892	-0.0364	1.6873	-0.0579
9	1.148	0.1342	0.9918	1.7307	1.0115	-0.036	1.5758
10	1.148	1.3142	0.9918	-0.1288	0.2583	0.0436	0.3051
11	-0.6777	0.5602	-0.7191	1.9897	2.3904	-0.0068	-0.4639
12	-0.1545	0.1918	0.1674	-0.8815	-0.81	-1.4595	-1.1292
13	0.2352	0.1735	0.9918	-0.3942	-0.019	-0.4104	-0.5878
14	-0.1545	0.1735	0.1674	-1.1284	-0.423	0.0436	-0.1593
15	0.2352	-0.1939	1.1624	0.6379	2.4357	0.8981	1.1043
16	-1.5906	-0.948	1.038	0.369	0.4051	0.2502	0.3197
17	0.3687	-0.5806	0.6107	-1.1124	-0.6151	2.7675	0.8687
18	1.148	1.3142	1.4351	-1.3712	-1.1213	0.3018	-0.9184
19	-1.3235	1.3142	-0.781	-0.1857	-0.6632	2.7017	1.1872

Net step is to move this kept data and insert them to the original dataset (perhaps the backup file). And convert the file to CSV format.

And then, open a new model in PLS, while this time, just assign the new set of indicators to the model.

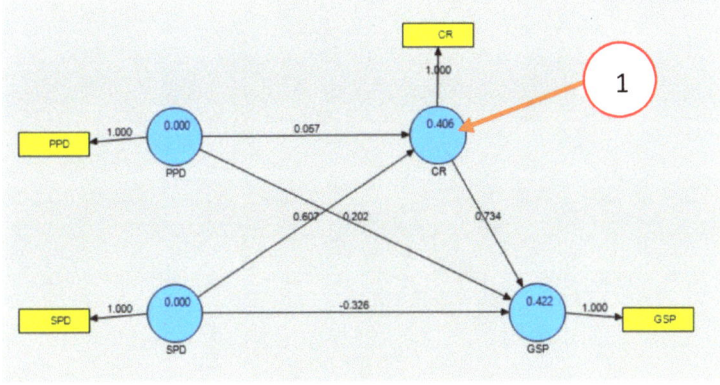

49 | P a g e

noted that, the factor of "Collaborative Relationship" was the second order in our first phase of analysis, while now in second phase it convert to first order though carry those second order formative values.

Next screen shot is the bootstrap of the model, which indicates the significance of these relationship.

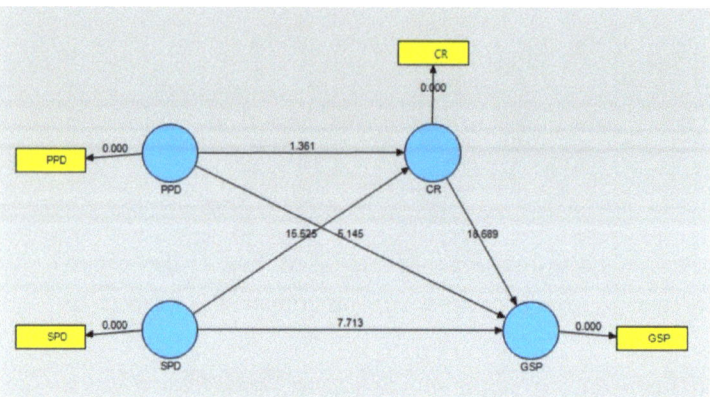

Chapter 8

Multigroup Moderation and Moderated Mediation

Learning Objectives:

This chapter offers understanding about:

- Step-wise process of multi-group moderation and mediation

For analysing the multi-group moderation and mediation, let's consider the example of social science research about youth risk behaviour. The research framework is presented in next and here we consider the question of 'if the effect between psychological factors and youth risky behavior is significantly difference between males and females'.

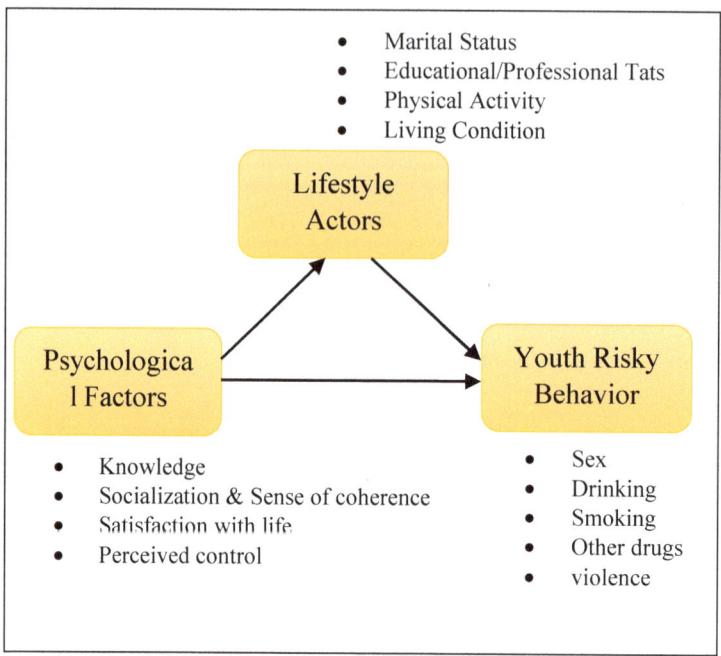

i) Multi-group Moderation

In version 2.0 of the SmartPLS it is not designed this function to do analyse between groups and therefore, in order to analysis the multiple moderation we need proceed few steps.

The first step is preparation of dataset. It begins with splitting the SPSS data into two files of males and females. The procedures is:

Data → Select Cases

From the windows of "select cases", first we need to select the "if condition is satisfied" and by click on option of "if" the windows of "select cases if" will appear. And here we need to define "Gender = 1" for the male and click on continue.
The next, is to save the file. So, in section of "output" we need to select the option of "copy selected cases to a new dataset" and name our new dataset. For example I define it as "Males for PLS". And then "ok" and now we have a new dataset.

Note that, this new file is not saved and we need to save it in both format of SPSS use (sav) and as well as PLS use (csv).

Exactly same steps, should proceeds for splitting the dataset for the gender of female.

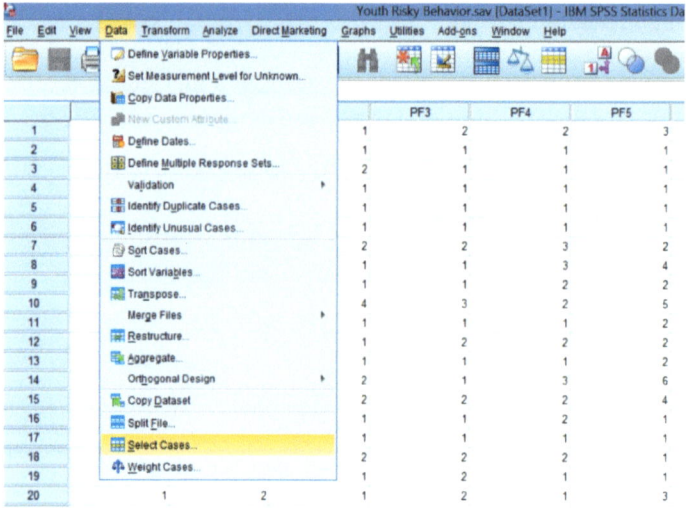

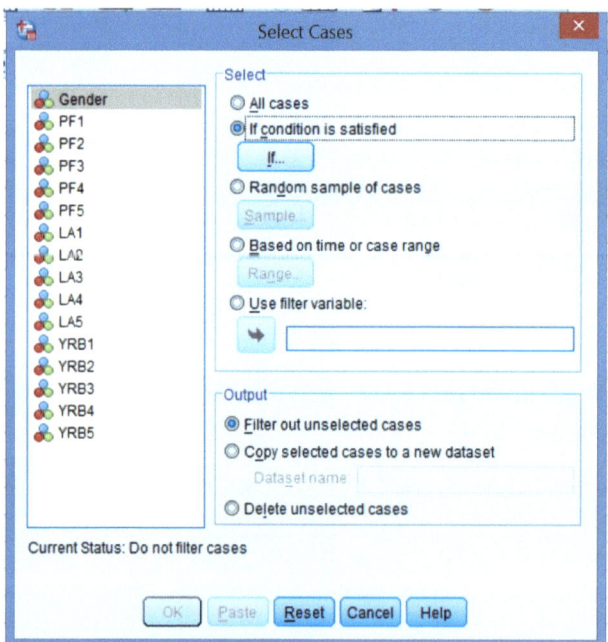

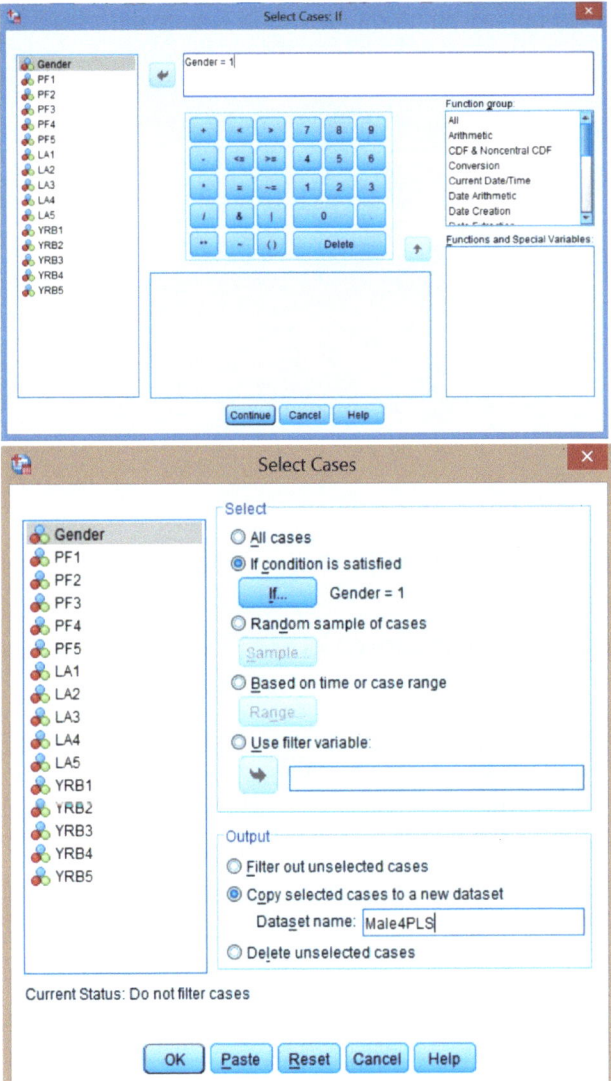

The next step is to upload both new male and female datasets into the PLS model.

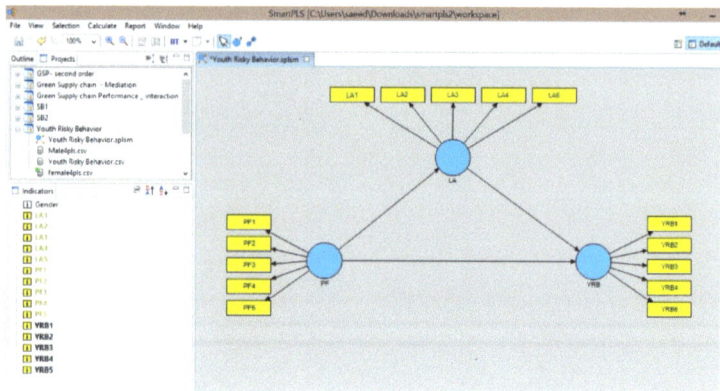

The next step is to find out whether the effect changes in different datasets.

The next screenshot shows the effect of "PF" on "YRB" for whole dataset.

PLS Algorithm	Bootstrapping
As we see the effect is 0.40 which is high	For the bootstrap there is not much significant effect as t-statistic of 0.459 is less than 1.96 significant at %95 of confidence level.

56 | Page

The next screenshot shows the effect of "PF" on "YRB" for the males.

PLS Algorithm	Bootstrapping
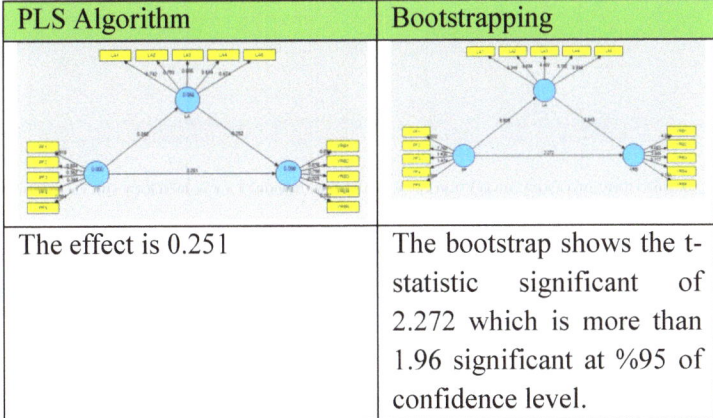	
The value is negative (-0.193) which is substantially lower than female	Here also the t-statistic of 1.218 is less than 1.96 significant

And the next screenshot shows the effect of "PF" on "YRB" for the females.

PLS Algorithm	Bootstrapping
The effect is 0.251	The bootstrap shows the t-statistic significant of 2.272 which is more than 1.96 significant at %95 of confidence level.

Through executing the PLS we noticed the values given for female and males are different. But to interpret if statistically the males are different from females, we need to do some calculation for example using the formula of Chin (2000) to calculate the t-statistic.

$$t = \frac{Path_{sample\_1} - Path_{sample\_2}}{\left[\sqrt{\frac{(m-1)^2}{(m+n-2)} * S.E._{sample1}^2 + \frac{(n-1)^2}{(m+n-2)} * S.E._{sample2}^2}\right] * \left[\sqrt{\frac{1}{m} + \frac{1}{n}}\right]}$$

To obtain the data, after bootstrapping, and from the 'default report', we choose the output result of 'Path coefficient (Means, STDEV, T-Values)'.

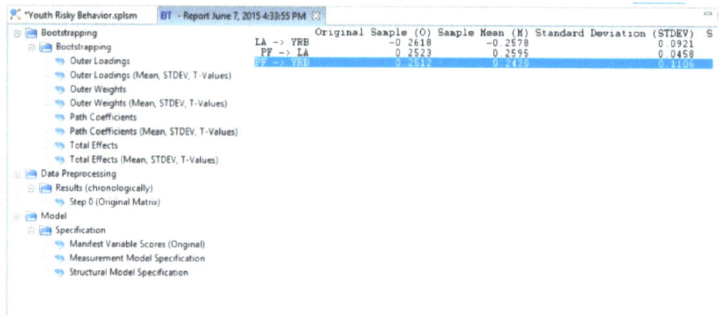

For female the sample means or the average estimate of 81 cases is 0.2430 ; with Standard Error of 0.1106.
For male the sample means or the average estimate of 89 cases is -0.0441; with Standard Error of 0.1611.

By assigning the data into the formula, we will have the t-statistic of 1.450 which is less than 1.96 significant at %95 of confidence level of 2 tail probability of 0.149 or 1 tail probability of 0.074.

so we can say with %95 of confidence there is no much difference between female and male in term of Psychological Factors and Youth Risky Behavior , while the effect of female is stronger than males (regression weight male -0.0441 < female 0.243).

ii) Moderated Mediation

Let us consider the previous example of 'Youth Risky Behavior'. Here we want to know the mediating effect of 'Lifestyle Actors' between two variables of 'Psychological Factors' and 'Youth Risky Behavior' and it's different between male and female.

The process is same as before, but after bootstrapping, and from the 'default report', we need to choose the output result of 'total effects (Means, STDEV, T-Values)'.
Here the result for female the sample means for 81 cases is 0.1770; with Standard Error of 0.0952.
For male the sample means for 89 cases is -0.0421; with Standard Error of 0.1574.
Similarly we use the formula of calculating t-statistic developed by Chin (2000).

$$t = \frac{Path_{sample\_1} - Path_{sample\_2}}{\left[\sqrt{\frac{(m-1)^2}{(m+n-2)} * S.E._{sample1}^2 + \frac{(n-1)^2}{(m+n-2)} * S.E._{sample2}^2}\right] * \left[\sqrt{\frac{1}{m} + \frac{1}{n}}\right]}$$

By assigning the data into the formula, we will have the t-statistic of 1.170 which is less than 1.96 significant at %95 of confidence level of 2 tail propability of 0.244.
So we can conclude that, the total effect of 'Lifestyle Actors' and 'Youth Risky Behavior' including the effect of 'Psychological Factors' is statistically not different between males and females ; while the effect for female is stronger (Regression Weight male -0.0421 < female 0.177).

Reference

Adèr, H. J., Mellenbergh G. J., & Hand, D. J. (2008). Advising on research methods: A consultant's companion. Huizen, The Netherlands: Johannes van Kessel Publishing. ISBN 978-90-79418-01-5

Chin (2000). Frequently Asked Questions – Partial Least Squares & PLS-Graph. Available from: http://disc-nt.cba.uh.edu/chin/plsfaq.htm (accessed 21-02-2007).

Index

Cross Loading (30,31,32,63)
First Order (46,50,63)
Interaction Moderation (35,36,38,63)
Mediator (41, 44, 63)
Outer Loading (28, 30, 63)
P-Value (23,63)
Second Order (45,46,48,50,63)
Structural Equation Modelling- PLS (1,63)
Correlation (3,19,63)
Formative Constructs / Formative Model / Formative Structure (2,3,4,27,33,45,46,50,63)
Moderated Mediation (51,60,63)
Sobel Test (39,40,43,44,63)
Modelling (1,12,13,14,67)
Multigroup Moderation (35,51,52,53,63)
SmartPLS (4,53,63)
Latent Variable (2,47,48,63)
Reflective Constructs / Reflective Model (2,3,4,27,33,63)
Constructs (1,3,4,27,45,63)
CSV Format (8,49,63)
Factor Weights (33,63)
Analysis (7,9,13,16,17,18,25,26,32,34,37,39,40,50,53,63)
PLS Algorithm (17,18,27,37,40,41,46,56,57,63)
Bootstrapping (17,19,20,21,22,38,40,42,44,56,57,58,60)
Factor Loading (30,33,63)

End

This book is a reader-friendly and very easy to follow for those who intend to familiarize themselves with data analysis methods. For research students, this book will provide guidelines on how easy and systematic use of statistical program of SmartPLS. Statistical technique used in the form of SmartPLS program professionally designed to estimate the variance-based structural equation.

Though the latest version of SmartPLS 3.0 is available for research fellows, and it is very much recommended by authors to advantage the latest version of this program, nevertheless, this book is written based on the previous version of SmartPLS 2.0 which can be obtained free of charge at www.smartpls.de.

The structure of this book is designed systematically begins with an a quick tour of screen , modelling and assigning data , executing (running) the analysis , factor analysis , moderation analysis , mediation and sobel test , 2nd order formative constructs , multi-group moderation and moderated mediation and how to make the reporting of the study.

This layout is easy to follow by those involved newly with the analysing research. In addition, narrative and simple language uses in this book, along with in-depth explanation of the concept using different example and set of data, helps readers within different levels of proficiency to understand the techniques and execute in their own research with confidence. Therefore, one can say, this is a real handy guide edition of statistical analysis using SmartPLS.

Cover image/Design: © Saeedeh Fattahi

First edition 2014
Published by: Eastland's Science Ambassador

www.ingramcontent.com/pod-product-compliance
Lightning Source LLC
Chambersburg PA
CBHW041204180526
45172CB00006B/1190

284 Ramsay Street – 1840 – Georgian – Frank Kehl residence

291 Murray Street – corner quoins

298 Ramsay Street – Gothic, shed dormers, decorative wooden porch supports – John Askin/Hamilton House

302 Murray Street

296 Ramsay Street – Regency style - Berthelot Residence

296 Ramsay Street – Chittenden House - 1840

301 Murray Street – hipped roof, decorative wooden verandah supports, bay window on the side

312 Murray Street – Edwardian/vernacular

102 Gore Street – Gothic Revival, bay window, cornice brackets

107 Gore Street – pediments above doors- vernacular

109 Gore Street - pediment

193 Gore Street – Gibb House – 1837 – Gothic Revival

207 Gore Street – James Caldwell House

This original one-storey log house was built between 1835 and 1840 by James Caldwell. Caldwell served with the British Army during the Revolutionary War. At the end of this war, he was given a large tract of land in Amherstburg for his service. Georgian style

217 Gore Street – saltbox style – Ralph Jimmerfield Residence

225 Brock Street – St. John the Baptist Catholic Church - 1844
Lancet windows, buttresses, finials

Amherstburg was in its infancy when the first Catholic chapel was built on Bathurst Street. On May 1, 1800 Bishop Pierre Denaut wrote to Father Jean Baptiste Marchand (a Sulpician priest, pastor of Assumption parish at Sandwich) instructing him to "give as patron saint the name of St. John the Baptist." Crown land on Brock Street was obtained and in 1844 building of the Gothic edifice began. The bell tower was built in the late 1860s. In 1883 two stained glass windows, imported from Belgium, were installed. Eight more were added in 1894 and others in the early 1900s.

317 Ramsay Street – Christ Anglican Church – 1819

Christ Church Amherstburg was built on land donated by Colonel William Caldwell by the soldiers at Fort Malden in 1818-19 and is the original structure. It was one of the earliest Anglican places of worship in western Upper Canada. Its first service was on Dec. 12, 1819. Christ Church served the garrison at Fort Malden which was the base for the British from 1796 until 1851.

The kiss of the sun for pardon, the song of the bird for mirth,
One is nearer God's heart in a garden than anywhere else on earth.

266 King Street – former St. John the Baptiste Roman Catholic Parish School and Parish Hall –now Lighthouse Chapel Evangelical Baptist Church - 1875
Limestone – cobblestone architecture

246 King Street – Mount Beulah Church
Early school house known as King Street School with the purpose of teaching black students in the community

271 King Street - Nazrey African Episcopal AME Church
The Nazrey African Methodist Episcopal was built by Black refugees in 1848 – lancet windows – Gothic Revival style

277 King Street – Amherstburg Freedom Museum

Canada was a special place for Black refugees, where they could feel free after being enslaved for so long. This church symbolizes their hope of finally being respected and recognized as human beings. The Underground Railroad (movement of slaves from the United States to Canada in search of freedom) increased due to the British Abolition of Slavery Law of 1833 and the U.S. Fugitive Slave Law of 1850. Amherstburg was a critical entry point for fugitives escaping slavery by way of this Underground Railroad because of the narrow crossing point of the Detroit River from the United States to Amherstburg, Ontario, Canada. Bois Blanc Island served as a stopover point for some refugees before finishing the final leg of their journey to freedom.

Many Blacks put their skills to good use as sailors, prosperous farmers, innkeepers (William Hamilton), grocers (Henry Turner), millers (James Alexander) and shoemakers (Albany Pines). John H. Alexander was principal of the school for the Black community, later serving on the school board, town council and as town assessor.

289 King Street – 1½ storey Gothic Revival, board and batten, fish scale pattern on gable

281 King Street – dormer – Gothic style, shed dormers
1½ storey Cote-Simpson House – built about 1848
Log frame, brick construction, original clapboard siding

135 Simcoe Street – hipped roof, Italianate style

129 Simcoe Street – St. Andrew's Presbyterian Church
Lancet windows

Built in May 1846 - The Gothic wooden windows of the church were installed by soldiers of the Royal Canadian Rifle Regiment at Fort Malden.

"Forged Peace" – out of war, peace was forged

Commemorating 200 years of peace (1812-2012) and the longest undefended border in the world between Canada and our American friends

Commissariat Office – Callum Residence – rectangular brick bungalow with a low hipped roof and prominent end chimneys

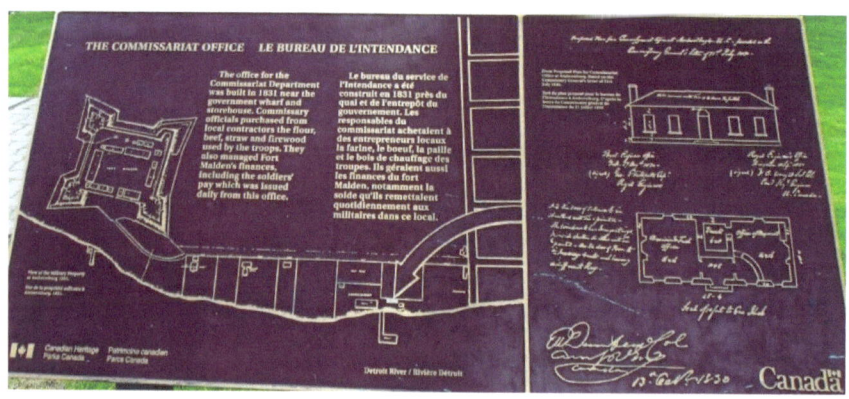

The Battle of Lake Erie

In September 1813 the British squadron under R. Barclay sailed from Amherstburg to collect desperately needed food supplies. They were met by the larger, more heavily armed American squadron commanded by O. Perry. The British had the initial advantage of the wind and used their long range guns to disable the American flagship Lawrence.

With his own ship crippled, Perry was rowed to the Niagara which had held back from the fighting. With the wind now to his advantage, Perry bore down on the British line pouring a murderous broadside into the enemy ships from his more powerful but shorter range cannonades.

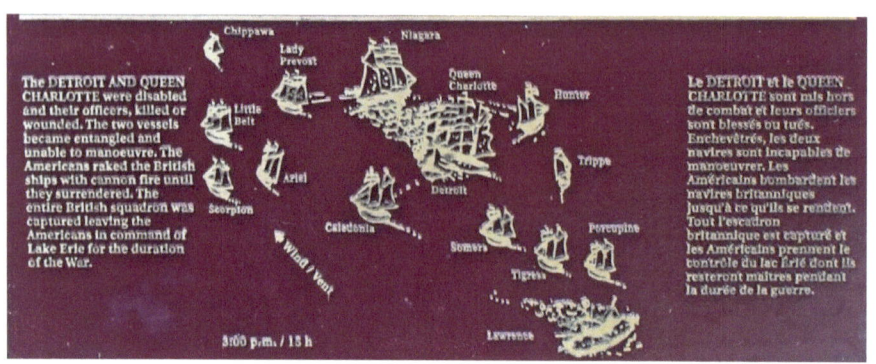

Artist Sculpture by Mark Williams – loading a cannon

Amherstburg Navy Yard was built here in 1796 to replace Detroit as the base and supply depot for the Provincial Marine on Lakes Erie and Huron. In 1812 the General Hunter and Queen Charlotte built here, took part in the capture of Detroit. The next year, his supply lines cut, Robert Barclayès poorly equipped fleet, including the Detroit, was defeated by Oliver Perry, U.S.N. in the Battle of Lake Erie. This reverse led the British to burn the Navy Yard on September 22, 1813 before withdrawing from Amherstburg.

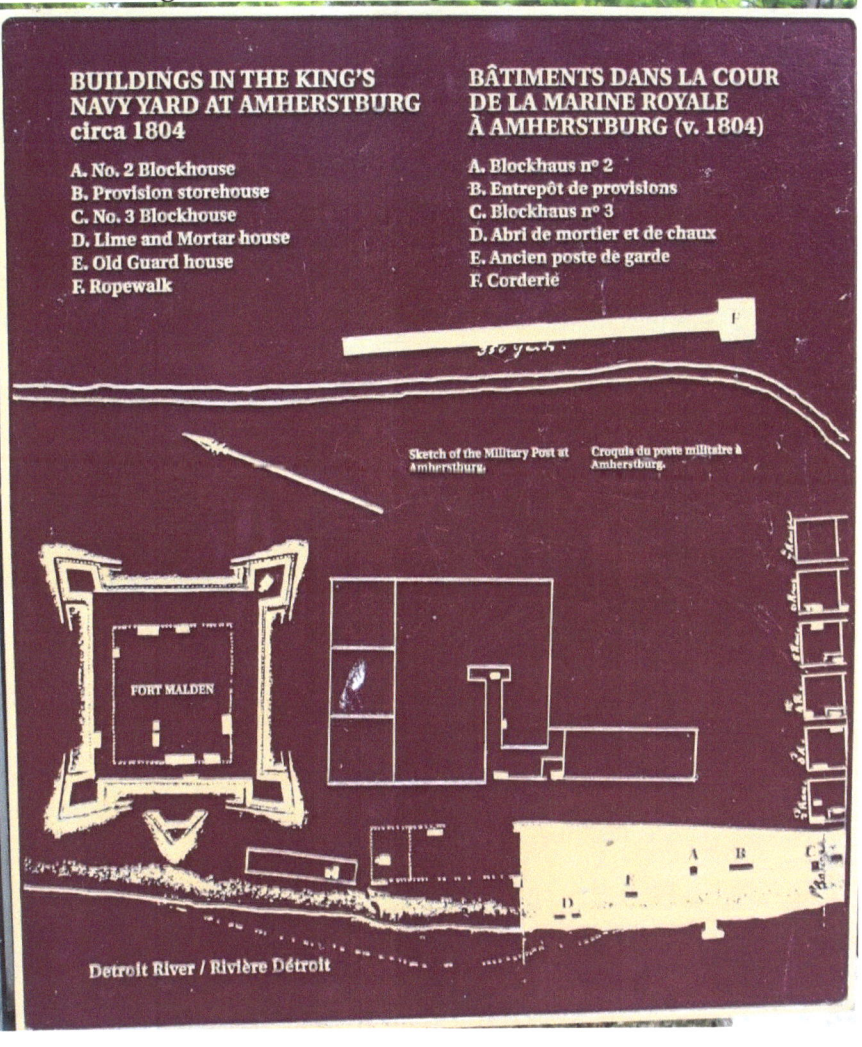

232 George Street – First Baptist Church – erected 1849 - one of the final stations of the Underground Railroad
Lancet windows

9399 North Town Line Road - St. Joseph Church - 1910
French-Canadian Church – a landmark at the centre of the former community River Canard
Entrance with Corinthian capitals on columns, voussoirs and keystones, decorative brickwork in gable

Buttresses

Town Line bowstring arch bridge over the Canard River

Architectural Terms

Bay Window: A window that projects out from a wall, in a semicircular, rectangular, or polygonal design. Used frequently in Gothic and Victorian designs. Example: 102 Gore Street, Page 15	
Brackets: a decorative or weight-bearing structural element which forms a right angle with one side against a wall and the other under a projecting surface such as an eave or roof. Example: 63-73 Murray Street, Page 10	
Buttress: a masonry structure built against or projecting from a wall which serves to support or reinforce the wall. In Canadian architecture, they are sometimes used for decoration. Example: 9399 North Town Line Road, Page 35	
Capital: The uppermost finish or decoration on a column. A Corinthian column is characterized by a rounded capital decorated with acanthus leaves and a square abacus (the uppermost portion of a capital directly below the entablature) on tall slender columns. Example: 9399 North Town Line Road, Page 35	

Cobblestone architecture: Refers to the use of cobblestones embedded in mortar as a method for erecting walls on houses and commercial buildings. Example: 266 King Street, Page 22	
Cornice: originally the wooden overhang of the roof. With the use of stone, brick, iron and steel, the cornice is any projecting shelf at the top of a ceiling or roof. They can be very decorative. Example: 63-73 Murray Street, Page 10	
Dentil Moulding: an even series of rectangles used as ornamental decoration in cornices. Example: 273 Ramsay Street, Page 10	
Dichromatic brickwork: the use of two colours of brick, tile or slate to decorate a façade. Example: 140 Richmond Street, Page 6	
Dormer: (French for "sleep") a gable end window that pierces through the plane of a sloping roof surface to create usable space in the top floor or attic of a building by adding headroom. Example: 298 Murray Street, Page 12	
Entrance: The entrance encompasses the doorway and the inner vestibule or, in residential architecture, the covered porch. Example: 9399 North Town Line Road, Page 35	

Gable: the triangular portion of a wall between the edges of a sloping roof. Example: 289 King Street, Page 26	
Hipped Roof: a roof where all sides slope downwards to the walls with no gables. Example: 301 Murray Street, Page 14	
Keystones and Voussoirs: a voussoir is a wedge-shaped element used in building an arch. A keystone is the central stone that locks all the stones into position, allowing the arch to bear weight. A keystone is often enlarged and embellished. Example: 9399 North Town Line Road, Page 35	church
Lancet Window: a tall, narrow window with a pointed arch at its top. Example: 271 King Street, Page 24	
Pediment: a triangular section above the horizontal structure (entablature), typically supported by columns. The inside of the triangle is called the tympanum. Example: 273 Ramsay Street, Page 10	
Pilaster: a slightly projecting column built into or applied to the face of a wall for additional structural support. Example: 63-73 Murray Street, Page 10	

Quoin: masonry blocks at the corner of a wall, often a decorative feature, usually larger or of a different colour than the rest of the wall. Example: 291 Murray Street, Page 12	
Rose Window: a circular window with ornamental tracery radiating from the centre. Example: 9399 North Town Line Road, Page 35	
Transom Window: the light above the doorway, also called a fanlight. Example: 273 Ramsay Street, Page 10	
Verge board and Finial: also called bargeboards – hang from the projecting end of a roof and are often elaborately carved and ornamented. **Finial:** ornament added to the top of a gable, pinnacle, canopy or spire – a Gothic element. Example: 259 Richmond Street, Page 9	
Window Hood: A **hood** is the piece found above window openings, usually of an ornate design, and covers the top third of the opening. Hoods are commonly placed above arched or curved openings on both windows and doors. Example: 63-73 Murray Street, Page 10	

Building Styles

Edwardian, 1900-1930 – This style bridges the ornate and elaborate styles of the Victorian era and the simplified styles of the 20th century. Balanced facades, simple roof lines, dormer windows, large front porches, and smooth brick surfaces are its characteristics. Example: 312 Murray Street, Page 14 (mixture)	
Georgian, before 1860 – This style began with the British King Georges in the 18th century. These buildings have balanced facades around a central door, medium-pitched gable roofs, and small paned windows. Example: 207 Gore Street, Page 17	
Gothic Revival, 1830-1890 – These decorative buildings have sharply-pitched gables with highly detailed verge boards, pointed-arch window openings, and dichromatic brickwork. It is a common style in Ontario. Example: 289 King Street, Page 26	
Italianate, 1850-1900 – It has wide-bracketed eaves, belvederes, wrap-around verandahs. Example: 63-73 Murray Street, Page 10	

Regency Cottage, 1830-1860 – This style originated in England in 1815 and spread to Ontario later in the 19th century as British officers retired to Canada. It is a modest one-storey house with a low-pitched hip roof and has a symmetrical front façade. Example: 296 Murray Street	
Saltbox: A saltbox is a building with a long, pitched roof that slopes down to the back, generally a wooden frame house. A saltbox has just one storey in the back and two stories in the front. The asymmetry of the unequal sides and the long, low rear roof line are the most distinctive features of a saltbox, which takes its name from its resemblance to a wooden lidded box in which salt was once kept. The earliest saltbox houses were created when a lean-to addition was added onto the rear of the original house extending the roof line sometimes to less than six feet from ground level. Example: 217 Gore Street	
Vernacular/Traditional Mode 1638 - 1950 Influenced but not defined by a particular style, vernacular buildings are made from easily available materials and exhibit local design characteristics. Example: 107 Gore Street	

www.ingramcontent.com/pod-product-compliance
Lightning Source LLC
Chambersburg PA
CBHW041113180526
45172CB00001B/234